Watermelon Rinds
&
Cherry Pits

Watermelon Rinds
and
Cherry Pits

Poems by

Murray Jackson

BROADSIDE PRESS
POST OFFICE BOX 04257
Detroit, Michigan 48204

ACKNOWLEDGMENTS

Some of these poems have previously appeared in
Renegade, Contemporary Michigan Poetry Poems From
the Third Coast, Callaloo, Peninsula Poets and
Woodland Sketches: Scenes From Childhood, by
Murray Jackson.
Cover design by George Lee
Illustrated by Arine Lewis

Constructive criticism came from Rudy, Steve, Alvin,
Saul, Gloria, Donald, Austa, Bernard and anyone else
who was in striking distance. The big support came
from the "group," John, Allison, David, Anne, Eugene,
Laura, Connie, Jennie, Bill, Kevin and Lisa. My
mentor, Laura, was the spark. Jennie, Eugene and
David, who read several manuscripts, contributed their
critical judgment and comments.

My friends in the Manuscript Workshop also gave me
support and counsel. A final thanks to my family who
put up with it all.

Library of Congress Catalog Number: 90-083555
ISBN: 0-940713-04-7

The words in this book are dedicated to Dauris, Llenda and David, with love and thanksgiving.

Contents

Growing Up Colored

Pull My Coat

Black On White

Letters from Poland — 'Dear Murray'

Ars Poetica

Introduction

Having already achieved full maturity, Murray Jackson encountered the Muse, and there began his passionate liaison with language, his restless desire to commit the very core of this pain and personhood to the page. So entranced was he with the magic of the craft that Murray confessed, "I covet the curve of new words."

Though this is the poet's first published collection, there are no "beginner's" issues here. Rather this poetry reflects several decades of a full, multifaceted life as husband, father, teacher, pensive observer of community life, lover. These are the notations of an urban villager who knows first hand the nooks and crannies of his people's life, and helps us to recall what has been forgotten, or imagine what we have never known. Here are remembered pool rooms and rent parties, con men and nuns in brown habits, strange in contrast with their ghetto surroundings. Here also are the poet's fine paintings of his beloved cityscapes. All of these images retrieve what has been lost in a eulogy almost palpable.

Following the poet's lead, it is as if we have come upon a family album of snapshots and portraits cataloging years of significant moments. Some figures are sepia-toned; others stand out in sharp relief, luminous against memory's backdrop. The poet smiles on all. No judgement is spoken here, only a wise soul's acceptance of life's disconcerting paradoxes *and* its miracles. We admire the poet's steady patience with life-as-it-is.

Open this book of pictures of the extended clan to which we all belong. Find yourself here. Inhale deeply the scent of memory.

Gloria House, Ph.D.   Detroit
Editor

Growing Up Colored

Growing Up Colored

The Old Boy walks from Canfield and Woodward
to Mansfield Highland Park Ford Plant
with Herman Davis, Sam Rustin,
looking to find Mr. Henry's man, Marshall,
who could say these boys are all right.

Pick-up men duck between
alleys and houses, not to get caught
to put your number in.
If you guess right, hoping that he
would hop, skip and jump to your
door with the hit money.

Trying to be the temporary weather boy.
look at the sky , scratch your head,
dig in your ass,
shuffle at the same time,
waffling through a minefield
of egg shells
You Got Rhythm.

Jabberwocking through the pains
of being colored.
Dancing sometimes,
even jitterbugging
through a Strauss waltz.

Friday night, rent party.
Was it going to be at Eva's again?
After, we could get to the fish fry
at Wimpy's.
Up all Saturday night.

Pray a little on Sunday.
Stand on tiptoes, straining to peer
on the other side of death.
Singing the edges of despair
with "Swing Low Sweet Chariot."
Monday, start to be colored again.

8 Ball in Side Pocket

Soft Side of Hastings, Oakland Avenue.
Wilfred's Billiard Parlor jammed between
The Pig Bar-B-Q and the Echo Theatre.

Slick Herman chalks his cue with resolution,
blue powder whispers to the floor.
He misses an easy bank shot in the corner.

Safe Eddie would always leave you on the rail
or hidin' behind balls you didn't want to shoot.
And steady Jerome looks for nonbelievers.
Hasn't missed a bank shot in four days.

Silent Ambrose shoots 9 ball
with Ralph, the Merchant.
Ralph accuses Silent of moving his balls
for a better angle, calls Silent a name.

Silent flashes quicker-than-light
2 inches of switchblade to Merchant's jugular.
In the stop-stillness of the moment,
you could hear a rat piss on cotton,
Don't you ever call me that . . . ever.

Silent wins the 9 ball game by forfeit.
Merchant can't find a cue
that will sit still in his hand.

Three Tone Poems for Unc Art Stelle

THE TIGERS

Frantic Ernie gave me my first baseball gloves,
maybe hoping someday he could see me play in Navin Field.
He took me to watch the Tigers.
Goose Goslin, Hank Greenberg, Charlie Gehringer,
Schoolboy Rowe,
Mickey Cochran, a prolific scholar on baseball,
always saying "If you don't like the Tigers,
you ought to move out of Detroit."
Saw the Tigers in '35, '45, '68,
and would have seen them in '84 if he hadn't
been so frantic.

THE ORIGINAL CONMAN

Living 52 years too soon, he could make
the sting feel like a butterfly,
never lost to work a deal.
Always had just enough change in his pocket
to give you 10¢ less than you asked for.
Nothing he didn't think he couldn't do
if he wanted to.
He thought he had the world by its pubic hairs.

THE PULLMAN PORTER

Railroad man from Dallas, Texas.
Travelled all over the country.
Stopped in Horseshoe Curve.
Knew as much about American geography as most teachers.
Could call train stops from here to Laramie, Wyoming,
without missing a beat.
Told us once that the engineer
let him drive the train for 15 minutes.

Baby Ray

Baby Ray cribbed on the blacktop
streets of Detroit
Scratched high honors at Southeastern.
His folks left for Vegas
to make it big.

"Someone To Watch Over Me,"
which he used to hum all the time.
"Won't you tell her please
to put on some speed?"

We used to call him "Mooch" cause
he was always on "e", not anymore.
Raymond found the fast lane.
His street cabinet helped.

Wolf, the con man for all seasons,
Fast-break Benjamin always in foul trouble.
Bee, her dime-sized waist and healthy hips,
Stu the police advisor,
Phil the soothsayer of John R.

Early mornings Pindillys to play 21.
If the cards fell right all
hustlers in the joint got gappers.
A fresh start tomorrow.

The Cakewalk Shuffle to the Frolic where
Arnett Cobb was working out. The Garfield
Lounge for chicken in the basket.
If action was still acting,
on to Sassy Sarah at the Flame.

Ladies of Josephat

They walked the mortared brick of St. Antoine,
high-top shoes laced all the way up, onto Beaubien
where the street car ran. Beaded and cross-chained,
they lockstepped from the sand red-walled-chapel
of St. Josephat, past the three copper-colored
iron balls of the pawn shop, down to our block,
across Brush to Canfield.

It was whispered around that they were
witches and gypsies, from the old country.
I didn't know any better.
Struck dumb, I just watched them.
Celled in brown and white habits,
their dark vanilla faces smuggled out
smiles, as they walked past us.

From the gait of their steps, I thought
I heard an old spiritual chant
first remembered in a sanctified
storefront church on Forest Street.

YES, I BEAT THE DEVIL RUNNING
AND I'M ON MY WAY TO HEAVEN
AND THE WORLD CAN DO ME NO HARM.

Sledge's Barber Shop

Mr. Clay Sledge from Tombigbee, Alabama,
just two cheeks of tobacco juice from the Mississippi,
had three chins, working number four.

You could tell that few servings of hot,
brown corn bread, chittlins, greens
and neck bones got past Clay Sledge.

The shop was clean, spittoons polished most of the time.
When me and my brother went to the barber shop
Mr. Sledge needed no instruction, cue-balled again.

You could get your hair cut, and your shoes shined sometimes.
If we listened hard, we
could hear a story or two about girls
and things we didn't understand.

But the men laughed, slapped their knees
and made funny noises.
You know what? The tale about the oldest profession,
it ain't true. The oldest profession is men lying to each
other in barber shops.

Racetrack Harry

My first real gleam of Harry
His sleeping place,
Library of Congress racing forms of yore,
True scholar any measure of the word,

Names leaped off bookshelves
Bearing down the stretch-run to the wire,
Man of war, Sea Biscuit, Citation,...
Arcaro, Hartack, Gurin, Longden,...

Harry was home — the track.
8 Mile Woodward — State Fair Grounds
Touts he brushed off, paid no mind
I watched, two-dollar investor hustlers

Bid against the world.
Think of them, real thoroughbreds.
Not the handsome, four-legged ones being stifled.
Held back by the whim of temporary masters

Kill-a-Rock Benjamin — didn't smile much
Stood for no messing around; got little inside information.
Like a dealer from Vegas,
Ashcan Alexander could flip tickets
Abandoned after races hoping to find a live one.

Fast Benny took buttons off your shirt
Faster than a seamstress; never said excuse me.
Gorgeous Mamie fine as she wanted to be.
Fully furnished — Better Homes could do no better.
A stone fox.

Miss Lucy

Squash yellow pieces of paper
crumpled twisted folded neat.
Picture albums before Kodak
Outdated dresses and hats
Clean pots, pans, and dishes.

Makes roast beef and rolls,
with the skill of a gifted surgeon.
Ten dollars on the dresser,
for anyone who needs it.

Gnarled hands wrinkled with wisdom
glide over washboards,
iron fine shirts, skirts, slips,
hot things in and out of stoves
dust mopping white folks
so they'll be presentable to each other.

Shoes overrun and out, squeak
with her rhythm
as she makes it everyday.

Two nephews, Playboy, his Stetson hat,
pimp shoes stand spat on the corner,
twirls his key chain, looks for action.

Sam, Great Lakes Steel,
six children and Louise,
hides in the bicycle blues,
hopes to learn Georgia Skin.
Sweet Lucy, one line in the orbit column, Apartment 109.

Body and Soul

Coleman Hawkins, "The Bean"
recorded BODY AND SOUL,
1939 masterpiece
my kind of jazz.

MY LIFE A WRECK YOU'RE MAKING

Everyone waited for BODY AND SOUL
Time to coote across the floor slower than slow.

If Gwen was there,
the studs would break in her direction.

I only knew the two-step.
Still do.
The only dance I ever learned.

The two step
was born for BODY AND SOUL.
No light could creep between dancers' bodies
I'M ALL FOR YOU

To dance with Gwen was to go places
places you had never been
places softer than foam on beer.

I Got It

Just plain old black asphalt in America.
White bonnet broad brimmed
Ribbons the color of royalty
Push cart dressed all up
Rainbow sheets
Big sign red and white
I got it.

City street Gypsy selling his wares
Skillets, pots — an almost cashmere sweater
Crooked label from Saks
Bent bicycle wheel shining like a new dime
A real pearl necklace — zircon diamond rings
From the Five and Ten six rolls of Louie XIV wallpaper
Two bottles — Nature Boy — Cadillac Club
One half empty one half full
Out of the sides of his mouth

If I ain't got it today
I'll have it tomorrow
Tell me what you need
I got it.

Dudley Randall

Pushed through a crack in earth
your eyes burn fire, soft as soft
your vision of cities: Green Apples, Roses
and Revolution.

You find the green moss discover north
tie square knots to hold our world together
press the pressure points to keep us
from bleeding on city streets.

In Paradise Valley, your man
Caruso flashes the ruby stick-pin,
stands on his chair
talks about being colored.

Prophet Jones sashays
to his temple on Hague.
Floats to the pulpit in his ermine robe,
Hands outstretched for alms.

Casablanca shadows Orchestra Place,
touts his basement palace, a place to look at cards,
have a taste or two.

You catch the mellow harmony
of their beat
siphon time, bottle it, then
uncork and stick it in our eye.

Some Streets in My City

The country Club Barthwell Drugs,
Canfield and Brush.
Largest ice cream cone in America
for five big ones 5¢.

Membership open to all! Listen
Willie the Pimp and Cadillac Bill,
discussing ways to spot the man
in order to stay loose.

To live in the city is to be smart
and dumb among all things.
To roam the streets, unscarred
not possible — alive but scarred.

Unfunny streets — funny people
sirens whistle the song of promise,
untutored but schooled to life
that lets them survive.

Games played in the streets
Three Card Molly, Georgia Skin
one huge Shell Game
That gets us all.

The color of streets change.
Are we swift enough to understand
before the hurt gets us?
Do we have time to check the Sanskrit?

Semi hip street-wise hustlers
live in the city.
Don't even know their ass
from a manhole cover.

Baby Ray, my main man
His place, The Bamboo Room
Not very legal, lots of action.
One day he left somethings with a man
to help pay for my learning.

Paradise

The eruption sloshed
the corridors of Old Main.
Truth and Beauty were done, another week.
Friday, 4:15.

Delores and Julia wanted to take me to Paradise.
How do you get to Paradise?
I've never been.

Take the streetcar down Woodward to Selden,
past the Graystone Ballroom, Majestic Theatre,
the prison flanneled National Bank of Detroit and
the orange painted second-hand bookstore.

High yella Delores with garden green eyes
reaches still higher.
Always seemed to look for a seance to happen.

Julia wore her paradise dress
that grabbed her secure all over.

She didn't stop time when she walked,
she just created motion and deep froze it.
The seams of her dress overflow just enough
to let you know what they were holdin'.
. . . Big gams too.

Go to the top balcony of Paradise.
Lady Day looking for "Lover Man."
"Flying Home" Hampton,
Dinah, "Ain't Nobody's Business If I Do."

When I go back to paradise   Orchestra Hall
hear the Guarneri Quartet,
the Detroit Symphony,
I look to the top balcony.
I still hear Diz, Count, Bird, and
Mr. B's "Cottage for Sale."
You know what? I betcha Julia is still freezin' things.

Out of My Window

The oyster shadow sky coughs red orange
fire that tongues the morning, as white
incestuous clouds move together.
Ren Cen one large word processor never stops,
blinks messages back and forth from silver black ramparts.

Sand dune Blue Cross Blue Shield sits
patient and waits for another opinion.
1300 eyes Lafayette with quiet disdain as it
peeks from its penal colony gray wall.
Chrysler School trimmed in baby blue across
the top, beige bricks with light khaki doors.
Near the park with little slides and sand boxes,
hop scotch squares, grass to play on
trees and flowers to touch.

Medusa Cement twisting dull gray
tub building near the water for easy shipment.
Boat docks take on and put off.
The toes of Windsor touch the river
blue and red neon light - Home of
Canadian Club flashes on and off,
Then condos, apartments, office buildings,
hotels, strike new bright color
and some the same old stingy white.

The long smooth plate glass river stops
looks through itself then past the Belle Isle Bridge
and the cylinder stacks of the seven sisters.
Then Lake St. Clair drops to the end of the world.

The City

Trip hammers pound their calliope rhythms
tearing apart what was made to last.
Steam shovels clutch spoonfuls
of time from city streets.

Night hooded soft city shadows flush life,
camouflage creatures, flying things, even people.
Chimney smoke, drill presses
shaving to the bottom of the sky.

Always in labor, dimple stretch marks,
transplanted birth signs.
The funky sounds of streets
bulldoze us no matter what.

Expressways, parks and malls
Gold-plated homes platinum glass to see nothing
White-out the not possible
find the wizard of Delphi.

Human achievement from stinking little cities
not hillsides not forests and streams, but
rotten bickering crime-wrenched cities,
with fish markets, pawnshops, factories, street corners.

Cities—the toe jam of earth?

Pull My Coat

Pull My Coat

Reading a fist full of books
Two seminars on how to do it
Armed with backpack loaded with
everything including a thimble of air.

Everything fell into place
like green apples in springtime,
corn in summer,
hot biscuits and chicken on Sunday morning, but

One day I saw a withered elm,

and my beautiful calico cat, Taffy,
orange, black and yellow,
stopped swirling.

Our big black dog, Pepper,
stopped barking and howling
at things.

Help me remember.
Pull my coat.

II Poverello

My skin quivers firelight,
air stutters my windpipe.
I hurt as never before.

The flannel gray night seduced

I can't win your hand with knightly honor.
I must serve you, I am your servant.
Give all that I own, come bring nothing.
Not even self, just beggar stones.

You have signmarked them,
blotched demented skin, wrinkled,
arms and legs muted by the dull pull
of disgruntled muscles.

Time fits my hand.
I push from memory
the sharp jog of doubt,
You are all that I touch.

Press your flesh to mine,
So that I agonize with the same
Marks that bleed you.

Assisi, Assisi.

Caliban's Sonata

I am Caliban, giver of light.
Puppy-headed monster,
moon calf,
plain fish, natural man.

I bear wood to flame the light
for Prosper to hold the sea
and call Ariel to make music.

Tensions that tear make thunder.
Intestines turn and growl red,
the last nerve is frayed and pinched.
I grate against the time of rocks and earth.

Art survives when pushed and pulled.
Prosper, this thing of light,
I acknowledge mine.

Vermeer — Light Adagio

Unhusked seeds of white heat smuggled
polished in shadow-boxed windows
jabstalk the eye
bleeding color to visions of light.

Yarns of fabric loom bright fire
consuming quick as lizard tongue
timbres touch and trumpet sounds coil web
the ocular root tap.

Points of light dance the rhythmed stillness,
a gaze dissects depths of shadow
laser sharp flecks of bread and wicker for
what they are — nothing else.

The eye channel buckles, floods the lens
bright pale yellow, white blue gray
diffused, subdued, held captive by light.

Jupiter 41

Wrinkles of thunder ruffle strings
to the tall sound of dark bassoons.
Peach fuzz strains of gleaming
flutes pluck the air.

English horns genuflect
the sapphire ring of trumpets.
Mood and harmony modulate sparse
intervals that texture fire yellow.

The festive gossip of violins
swirls and pivots then serenades
the dark hush of oboes
fresh whispers of movement and rest.

Trumpets answer four beat phrases
An overgirth of sound,
soft in places not expected.
You listen to hear one mo'e time.

Serious Music

Frost-bitten fingertips clawing for warmth
Firelight that scorches, even consumes.
One large coke oven, like a saucer of blood
running, raging red against the sky.

Tearing from their souls to create—
Mozart, Beethoven, Bach.
Intent to reveal the depths of whatever
made them search for music and words
Duke, Bird, Trane, Fats.

All looking in the same places for pieces of light
locked behind unlocked doors.
Shredding veins, marrow
all else necessary to be makers.

Mozart, Ellington, Fats,
Even the Cantor of Leipzig
Press their noses against the
looking glass hoping to see.

Night Chain

Extended hands with purple plums
shine in the half light of night and
reflect the glare of patent leather.

The long sleeves of night reach
to find nightmares to pour—
we all stand in a circle and wait our turn.

Transformed bodies transfixed to life
limp dishrags unfurl dreams, nerves
spread the pain to faces that split from self.

Under the lid of dusk sleep dancing in New Zealand
to the beat bells that whisper the death of a monarch,
from Westminster towers a victory long forgotten.
Shona drum bells of Zimbabwe — a new beginning.

Sleep on pillows of elephant tusks
wrapped in sheets of wild boar's hair
from the deep dream of night, we roll ourselves
into balls and hide in our own shadows.

Lee

Hanging fire from their lips
Cass Warren coffee and talk
A smile that knew before you knew
hacking laughter, tall and straight,
short cropped black hair
dark eyes that never turned off.

She pricked my hand with
Gammer Gurtons Needle.
Told me about good ole Beowulf
in a musky place looking for Grendel
the big-headed monster
and his vengeful mama.

Lee, I will rehearse your memory
when the breath of summer
pushes young leaves and sweet vapors
and when damp scholars with the
quick hands of impatient lovers
revisit Shakespeare's place.

Then I will think of Edmund's
Faerie Queen with her Red Cross Knight.
Robert Greene with three E's
the lusty days of winter on the corner
of Collingwood and Hamilton as we
waited for the bus to campus.
The small tidy in-between days
when you and Chet would help us
resurrect a thought or two
with your Old Taylor and our water
now ambushed by swift footed time.
I touch books and things you left.

Gathering

Me and my little brother "Babes" are thoroughly baptized
in the bathtub by Mom Saturday night.
Sunday morning, Second Baptist Church, Monroe Street
we ride the Beaubien streetcar all the way downtown.
The conductor with his stingy-brim cap
flips the seats North for the trip back.
I grumble to Sunday School and sometimes church
to hear Reverend Bradley preach about the Spirit
and Frederick Douglass who came to talk here once.

The Amens are done, we are on our way
back to Canfield, fried chicken, crisp brown and hot,
white rice piled high next to steaming collard greens.
Hot biscuits thirsting for margarine colored the night before.
Then waste the rest of the day
scraping, washing dumb ol' dishes, pots and pans.

I Too One Day Will Die

I too one day will die
Will it be on some dark stinking street
Running horizontal to the rest of the world?

For certain, no marble hall or sacred place.
Should it be in my city that I have loved
Ever since I walked summer sidewalks,

Rat infested, garage laden alleys
that served as playing fields of Eton
negotiating ice when Hawk was taking names?

Maybe on the hillside, flowers, grass,
Even weeds struggle for life, overlook my world,
help me remember what it was, and never was.

There will be no flashing lights crescendo of music—
Bright sounds come when we celebrate
The living of life.

Black on White

Boston 36 Floors Up

Sullen river pouts in a corner
caught in the winter arm-lock,
our side of the Charles,
a picture of 18th century London.
Houses stuffed like sausages
about to split.
Stacked stack on stack.
On the other side towers, temples,
townhouses and shrines.
Bird creatures on ice floes,
bridges that escalate cars
into the 20th century.

In an eye flicker
the sun flashes reflections
on both sides of water
like Dali
flaunting lightfire.
Cans of light
show things the sun left out.
Across the river one large
computer print-out
black and white.

Tampa Gull

Yellow-nosed herring gulls
sculling the sky
looking for alms on water, waste dumps
even black-top parking lots
wherever there is a handout

Whispering in the eardrums of air

Hiyah   Hiyah   Hiyah

Moving with the rhythm of a smooth slick piston
in unison with the glide of grease on grease.

Robert Brown Elliott

How my voice excites the morning
as I thunder in the halls of Congress.
The dark-eyed stare that is mine alone
stops motion when I fight for South Carolina.

As I listen to the gentleman from Sumter,
I should be derelict in my identity
if I remain in my seat.
I know I frustrate nerves.

Me, Robert Brown Elliott, indentured to none,
Honors — Eton; Law — the King's Council.
My bloodline runs through the Indies
My place of birth, Boston.

They will honor and respect me
because I am more than equal
to any of them on any occasion.
Only if I could be less uppity.

It was the Irish
imported from Ireland
men from the swamp and bogs
responsible for the change in suffrage.

I am not Othello
disenchanted by imperfection
or the black-faced minstrel player who
sings, bows, dances! I am none of these.

I squat, contemplate the low-hanging blue-eyed sky,
outraged with its own infidelity.
In search of old victims for new atrocities,
in the name of some god colored white.

My disabilities do not allow me
to be corrupted by the corruption
of others, my vision is not deformed.
Yet I am all of these things;

Different times different places,
but I alone decide when and where.
I may be between dreams,
when between dreams choices are few.

New Freedom Fighter
Angela Futch

Chapel in the rain.
Angela found herself sitting, listening to the sound
of history echo from ceilings, walls,
voices of old freedoms.
DuBois - Booker T. - Douglass
Spattered light through the colored glass
bouncing off blurred rain the stench of
freedom mixed with blood, anger,
burning flesh, twisted bodies.
5th of March, 1770. Little Rock, Montgomery, Selma.
Angela marching, standing up in footpaths
necessary for freedom.
Listening to the tape of John Coltrane,
new freedom fighter.
No wrong in that, even in the chapel.

Pigeon-Toed Knock-Kneed

Going with the pitch from first to third
infield hit, molasses rolling over pancakes.
Flatbush, Ebbets Field, the real Dodgers
Erskine, Campanella, Peewee, Newcombe, Hodges.

The Giants' pitcher attempts to rearrange his rib cage
and help with double vision.
Jackie would drop a bunt soft caramel on Cracker Jacks
seducing the pitcher to field the ball,
ripping down the first base line,
he always came ready to play.

You sensed the built-in range from Alabama, UCLA
Army, Montreal, now the Brooklyn Dodgers
coming from all the playing fields
being spit at, cursed, niggered at,
he came to play and did.

Opening day Ebbets Field pumped up, inflamed
waiting for the ump to give the word.
First the Anthem in his private space
The soul's wounds now he knew, were worth it all.
His blue cap over his heart
"The home of the brave, land of the free."

No Ebbets Field, no place to reminisce
but his name is carved in base paths,
Yankee Stadium, Wrigley Field, Forbes Field,
and in a place called Cooperstown.
What do we owe Jackie Robinson?
To remember the struggle against the current,
is not to ask but — to demand.

ANEB Kgositsile - Gloria House

When we are laid
in the dust covering ourselves,
even in death we create:
Trees, plants, worms, snakes,
bees, flowers, fleas and epitaphs.
Rubbing on marble
sand and dirt,
The poet —

Freibürg

Angles of orange-topped roofs
houses tighter than Siamese shadows
defiant, motionless, an extended family.

Enclosed, shaped spaces, green
onion-topped turret buildings, churches,
seems they all want to belch a Wagnerian aria.

Market in the church square the cathedral,
twelfth century overseer watching, listening, giving sanctuary
to the bells as they strike the word.

As I jogged the park, red-pink flowers
playthings for children, almost life-size
orange and white chess players.

Ducks, geese, all kinds of birds
World War I monument in honor
of the 173rd Regiment.

Outdoor stage reading some Shakespeare,
I gently roared across the stage,
in Freiburg — what a thrill.

I could hear, "Who is that man —
athlete, TV star, used to be a fighter?"
Startling them.

"Guten Morgen, schoner Tag,
Wie geht's, auf Wiedersehen!"

A Walk in the Black Forest

All decked out, fields of green and yellow
manicured, pedicured to disbelief.
Mountains of granite raised
hiccupping earth's belly spasms.

Herds of green-black pine trees
dinosaurs grazing the sky.
Houses that start below dirt,
roofs that touch the ground.

Splashes of fog spray
water gouge-claws, and thrashes new
cylinders of sound
a giant afterbirth, the Danube.

People plant and harvest
dressed to show their place
of work and birth
time is a long — goodbye.

Detroit-Chicago Train Time

Michigan Central railroad station,
ancient Greek temple Doric columns
Corinthian cloisters.
The walls and floors could sing
had they voices.

World War II troop trains from all over the country,
stopping for a moment at Michigan Central.

From the station to the train yard reminds you
Frankfurt, 1944-45.
Twisted pieces of concrete and steel like black
and red licorice.

Yards of junk, pieces of brown-green machinery
Houses that sit and look at you through dirty windows.
Yards back and front stuffed full of cots, chairs,
ovens, refrigerators.
Yes, a portable swimming pool.

Fields of corn,
some cabbage,
cows slapping air in search of flies,
horses ogling grass
19th century railroad stations
Niles, Kalamazoo, Jackson.

My friend and colleague, Cleo Harpoon,
working her treatise "The History of Junk," might
find this route ideal for a museum
on everything nobody wants.

Naked October

Swashbuckling bright colors
the hue of burnt orange,
gold and yellow marmalade.

Slinking around corners
hiding in the closet of August,
Slip sliding to the ground.

Go naked to Earth,
the quilted blanket protects.
The next sunrise choreographs
the rite of passage.

Letters From Poland ---
'Dear Murray'

I

What kind of wishes shall
I send you?
I wish for your unfulfilled dreams.

Yes, I wish you that.
Your peaceful nature touches
others
as it has me.

Unsure about coming home.
Maybe I stayed away too
long.
Still don't know what I am
yet.

II

Maria Sklodowska University, Lublin.
Fight for bottled milk, no bread, little soap.
Polish workers become migrants.
Go pick grapes in France and Greece.

I like "Kirsten" and "Bus Stop"
DSR smells associated with warm weather,
city perspiration, alcohol breath, whisps of
cheap sweet perfume.

I will use your poetry in my class.
Your vision is so full of possibilities.

III

Tensions in June
Solidarity increasingly active
Creates movement that involves me.

Special permit needed for meetings.
Some of us are involved.
All are not.

Lech Walesa shakes his fist at the air
Captivating, forceful. When he speaks,
you hear the clock in the town square.

IV

Revolution still brews here, University strike.
Blue-jeaned students man the administration building.
Staying the university 24 hours.

Scratch out mini kitchens, sleeping bag row.
University curriculum is the fight.
General education requirements for what?

Tuesday sing-in.
Taught them to sing "We Shall Overcome."
Many already knew it.

V

Gdansk again.
I like this city.
I think I understand,
full of smoke stacks,
orange and white,
purple smoke coming from inside.
Green cranes that lift things
back and forth.
All kinds of people.
Homes rather dark and close
Same in Hamtramck and
Detroit.
Do I belong here?

Born in Detroit
Blood in Poland.

Ars Poetica

Ars Poetica

With no apologies to Plato or Marianne Moore,
I do like poetry.

To be able to appreciate whether the universe
swings from the left or the right
can be hot stuff
if you really know.

I covet the curve of new words
that rack the marrow.
Do I need a half-page footnote
in foreign tongues to tell me why?

You'd think some journals sociological
would be the place to discover
why prostitutes prostitute
and hungry mothers are malnourished.

But shadows come from real images, and
I need to know the color and feel of shadows.
If the poet is true and real,
I will inhale the image.

I don't want to listen to Beethoven
or understand what I have heard
through EEG Alpha Rhythms
as they beep the soundwave.

I must feel color; vitality of movement,
the force of sound through ears and eyes.
I carve new words from old,
touch the bone of meaning

I don't need a computer printout
to tell me what I've heard and seen.
I need the rhythm of poetry
that razors language to the quick.

Jogging Sherwood Forest

No band of merrymen, that was yesterday
just cars, people, trees, dancing pieces
of light shimmy through tree tops
on sidewalks, roofs and me.

Bluejays slapping the face of air
pirouetting with the wisdom of a
ballerina doing her thing
looking for cloud space, contemplating worms.

Long-legged blackbirds beeping
like antique seahawks
cardinals showing their colors
pigeons street smart, moving when they get ready.

Wet streets cultivate tree monsters,
leaping from the underworld.
Breaking tracks of snow on Sunday morning
to the Northwest territory —
Eight Mile and Canterbury.

Discarded crumbs from lovers' banquets
The Colonel, Big Mac
feed birds, squirrels, even raccoons
No Sheriff of Nottingham
Just plain old cops.

Whatyousee

I don't wanna survive
a long slow death march
castration by the numbers —
one hair at a time.

I will not be ignored —
I am not a second-hand pile
in the back room of a rummage sale.

Look the eyes of survivors, deep crankshaft
holes held together by gaskets of skin.
Eyes of tunnel light
that used to caress and seduce?

I do, I will
shout the life out of life
in my time
in my way.

Not by the whim of a nerve distracted
from its own reality.
No cellophane package of membrane
contrived to satisfy and please.

Mosaic

An instrument that startles birth
is more than rare
Co-maker of life.

Shutter-like flashes Cezanne landscape
Maybe we need to look again
I put words on paper.

Means I abandon nothing
helping to see what I thought better
maybe another way of finding.

Go to the top of Everest
Pick handfuls of snow my very own
Like a midwife holding hands with some god.

No one need tell me where I've been and
what I've done
Unafraid to touch to love is me I think.

How Can I Tell

Never thought I would know how
to talk to trees maybe I don't but
I'm gonna try.

I have when no one was listening
except maybe the damn ol' owl
on the tree stump.

Even if I had the strength
to turn God inside out
how would I know?

A seer of time
reader of leaves and hands
tell me what do the trees say?

Hidden in their bark and roots
going all the way to forever
Sometime we are stillborn and never know.

I Can't Pray for You

I pray for the woman child seven plus seven
carrying in her womb a heartbeat away
forced to succor life not understood

I pray for those who can't forgive
make no mistakes
for those who have never said I love you.

I pray for grizzly bears who will
destroy the world to save their little ones.
I pray for those who hate
they have no other energy.

I pray for waterfalls
Petite streams minuet from rocks
dirt and plants
snake dancing — to white thunder.

Pray for you, my friend?
Tell me how.

Two Friends:
Llenda, David

She is silver grace beauty
Seeing visions sometimes
forces her to look long deep,
her laughter that explodes

Shaking things in my head
So much like her yet so different
She has received many gifts
Sharing a place with us
Being herself what she is
leaves this to no question.

He gives me glimmers
            of myself
Determined to do what he thinks
            he must
Love with tender might
            knows no other way.

Patient thoughtful always in a slow hurry
He shows all who see the rock-like strength
Both endowed with what we had to give.

Knowing all about me
still insisting on being friends
You know what—I think they love me too.

Morning Star

Have you ever kissed the morning star,
Touched and held its caress,
Made love to the morning star?
Be not seduced by tender glances, future promises.
Beware, the morning star takes no prisoners.

Soliloquy

Come live with me.

Three women in my life
I have told I love
Trust me, trust yourself,

Don't be afraid to be warm
After love there's nothing
left to say.

Don't just say the words,
savor the naked taste of skin freeing itself
touching consuming lips and tongue

What we look for might be
sleepdriving on the freeway
without turn signals.

Unless we cling hard
as bark on trees

Scratching earth to earth
with fingernails and knuckles
ripped raw - we can't have it.

I asked you why you wanted to hold me, remember?
You said I consider things that matter, then do them.
Do it now — it matters.

Remember

Skin tight sounds haunt the night
heaving trucks and rolling tracks of trains
tugboats sigh and murmur in oil gray water.

Air turns green leaves to flashes of color
red, brown, beige paint the landscape
camera-like brush strokes.

Children dive-bombing their future with our past.
Crumpled yellow notes, funny lines, dashes, arrows
only we understand.

Squirrels in the big red oak play hide-and-seek
fetch leaves for a warm place,
even in snow.

As we fold ourselves into one another,
no matter how soft you leave,
I will think of you and remember.

Laura

Soft steam from a kettle in the kitchen
screaming gently, needs tending to.
Smell of fresh coffee, surf on the beach
Wind blowing the scent of rain.

Always trying to catch her breath
never having time.
Fighting to grab dreams
searching for things warm.

Maybe her child, Lydia
something to take a chance with
Honey colored fire red oak leaf
holding to the last.

Break dancing to earth
softer than fog dust
hugging mounds of dirt
rocks and trees.

Impromptu

The wine cellar.
Your apartment on the river.
The morning sun gushes tongue red
in the corner of sky.
We go see Purple, eat at the Michigan Inn.
Your twenty dollars helps pay for dinner.
I almost love you.

You take me to New York to meet
Charlie and Liz — surprise party for Liz.
We stay in Manhattan, Arnie's apartment,
eat at the Thai Restaurant around the corner.
Jog 57th Street on Sunday morning.
Street sleepers warm the sidewalks.

Walk Fifth Avenue holding hands
in the mild February rush of air.
Redecorate my house for the three of us.

Go to Bloomingdale's, I awe.
We buy French raisin cookies,
a bunny for Jason.

Sunday bus trip to New Jersey.
Brunch with Molly and Arnie,
walking on five acres of snow,
in the woods, warm thoughts even in cold
with your friends and you.

Collage

I first saw you on the street near the marketplace;
remember how the early sun rippled the transparent night?
And you kissed me on the cheek,
held me tight as skin on bone.

Don't hear me when I say wild flowers are
tucked in breezes, knots of clouds
hang together like pieces of popcorn, and
birds fly through clefts of sky.

I crowd on the back of stars
to see frost-bitten purple mountains in Madagascar.
I come to Timbuktu with its egg yolk yellow and
orange sand blowing back in the Niger.

Now I see you again, standing, smiling with open hands.
I press you in the lean pages of my book.
Wrinkled, limp, strange old men
still flame soft fire.

Touchword

Our sandpaper bodies,
skin armlocked to itself,
even pores resist one another.

I wrapped myself in the season of my love.
When the fall ritual shuffles through trees,
lights the flame
colors the leaf red yellow — then is gone.

If she ever loved me mouse toes on sand.
Quiet noise in the mouth of seashells.

I have counted the wrinkles on the face of the sky.
Dreams rejected by me
Never dreamt by her, how can I ask?

And yet, in her moontime,
Whenever she would hold me suretight,
close as flame in fire,
She never said I love you and I never asked.

Iliad

Looked lands older than time
Mountains flow to the Yang-tze
Called sometimes heard
whispers of silent thunder
felt warm tears of rain.

Visited the land of my fathers
Shona-stone builders maize gatherers
looking to see the
magic fire to tote away
lonely chills of night.

City roads lead vision untrue
myth makers shuck jive
like old ones before them.
Translucent lights, shiny people
dull my senses.

I found only you standing in sunlight.

August in Paris

The ship Casta Feliccia
North Atlantic leaping to touch the sky
White caps all over.

Holding hard, time wraps around rocks.
I shivered under discomfort, the ocean
Your tears on my chest.

Singing nursery rhymes on a little French street,
Playing with children dressed all in red,
Like cardinals marching in procession.

Walking from Mom Mom's on our way to
Sacre Coeur climbing a mountain of white steps.
Our second anniversary.

Paris Opera House columns of marble rich in ornament
Bronze gilt ostentatious Second Empire —
Ceilings painted in the grand style.

Facades lavish bright green and gold.
Rolling staircase of marble
Flowing to the Seine.

We were listening to Thais.
Looking at one another
Holding hands now and then.

I realized
Why I loved you.
Because of your fire-brown warm body

The mole that dances
When you smile
With your deep brown dimples.

The Scent of Memory

We walked Traverse Bay, kicking water at each other,
looking at a glass-bottomed sky.
Two people alone to ourselves in sand and water.

On the lake the smell of dogwood
scrubbed the dew, laughter rolled
over rocks and sand
searching for holes to push through.

Stacks of Petoskey stones ghost white
and night blue curled with each other.
The wet sand rolled off
our almost dry bodies,
brown sugar on cinnamon toast.

You smiled, orange light flashes against
a dull gray sheet.
The wisp of burned black coffee
is strong enough to resurrect anything.

ABOUT THE AUTHOR

Murray Jackson attended Wayne State University, receiving a bachelor's degree in Humanities and a master's in the teaching of College Humanities. His principal professional and academic interests deal with the politics of urban higher education. In 1980 he was elected to the Wayne State University Board of Governors. Jackson has been an active member of the Michigan Council for the Humanities and the Detroit Council of the Arts.